# Settlements

**Also by David Donnell**

# Settlements

# Settlements

## David
## Donnell

McClelland and Stewart

*The Canadian Publishers*
McClelland and Stewart Limited
25 Hollinger Road, Toronto M4B 3G2

*Canadian Cataloguing in Publication Data*

Donnell, David, 1939–
   Settlements

Poems.
ISBN 0-7710-2849-0

I. Title.

PS8557.05S4      C811'.54      C83-098765-7
PR9199.3.D6S4

The publisher makes grateful acknowledgment to the Ontario
Arts Council for its assistance.

Set in Mergenthaler Frutiger by Trigraph, Toronto
Printed and bound in Canada

*For my mother and my mother's
father Duncan*

The modern spirit became aware of its creative energies; it began to form and understand itself. The divergent and incoherent tendencies of the Renaissance were thus bound together by a superior intellectual force.

Ernst Cassirer, *The Myth of the State*


There's a slow train coming      and it's coming round the bend.

Bob Dylan, *Slow Train*

# CONTENTS

## Settlements

**American Buffalo Nickels**

# Settlements

## Beavers

The Hudson's Bay Company was an innocent philosophy school.
The beavers gave themselves up out of moral obedience.
The famous blanket they talk about was brought to Canada
by Scottish Diggers who became farmers until God
rewarded them with banks.

Buffalo Bill on the other hand slaughtered Dakota Buffalo
because he was American.
Because he had blond hair. Because he liked using a gun.
Because he was a drunk and they charged at him
like a brown wave every day when he went for a morning walk
across the plains.

Beavers have rich dark pelts.
Muskrats stink.
A woman who wears perfume made from muskrat glands
will attract strong men and experience unexpected pleasure.

The French win all the hockey games and eat glazed kidneys.
The Poles speak Polish and make buffalo vodka.

We are all innocent and guilty of everything under the sun.

Most farmers would rather trap otter or fox or mink.
Actresses wear blue silk underwear.
Trappers have red plaid shirts.
Stereotypes are wonderful because they make everything
                              as clear as road signs.
Moose is a delicacy. Blood is red. Daniel Boone shot bears/
while the Germans debated questions of philosophical method
America settled its west
the European peasants rebelled savagely again and again
and Sitting Bull came north because he believed in heaven.

## Satie at the Disco

He doesn't understand this music:
It sounds like nicotine and pernod—
not African so much as loud and hot

But lacking landscape. He walks
among the dancers on his way to the bar,
correctly dressed as usual,

And notices a girl in a white dress
shaking her hips and breasts like crazy
while a young man kneels at her feet;

His big Gallic ear, something like Gable's,
turns in the direction of the moon,
the ocean and the dark country,

Registers four or five of these notes
and bounces them, like bright ping-pong
balls, against the abstract wall of the sky.

# Making It in the City

*For Barry Callaghan*

Picasso lived for years on bread and ideas and bulls
and sold his drawings to friends. After he became famous
the gallery was besieged with thousands of buyers.
His social life improved. Clothing designers pursued him
all over Pigalle to give him expensive boat-neck sweaters.
Women threw themselves at his feet from behind closed doors.
Paris was open. Picasso's greatest early drawings
were of young boys leading horses out of blue space
and beatific couples making love in haystacks.

None of the women I know are throwing themselves at my feet
and the price of art materials makes supper impossible.
Only the pigeons outside Osgoode Hall believe in my kindness.
I wear the torn jacket and the white straw hat.
The blonde girl reading a novel thinks I'm a bum on welfare.
A breeze rustles her skirt, the pigeons lift, the streetcars
rumble by an old friend's bookstore and disappear in traffic.

I get in a cab with some Jamaicans and drive to the racetrack.
The evening races seem like a natural.
My form is marked up with a blueprint analysis of the fifth
and I have a tip from one of the trainers.
Franz Marc is on the other side of the Mutuals window
reading a French newspaper and smoking a short cigar.
He punches my rent money to win and smiles like a magistrate.
My horse gallops home at 99–1 and the track goes dark
except for the electric tote-board and the end of Marc's cigar.
I stand confused in the evening crowd
while several women throw their clothes in the air
and some pink underwear lands in my face.
I pocket the silk and listen for the announcer's voice.
It sounds like Mayakovsky and the saint says my horse is gone
'running in the milky dark beyond the wire'
across all fences into the blue and permanent fields of time.

## The Fire-Bombing of Dresden

These white-faced citizens of Dresden
haunt my library, caught naked, their shoes
kicked under the bed, penises swinging in the dark,

Thighs raspberry with flickering light,
jumping out of windows that no one has photographed
except flat and black with orange bursts

Shot from the air; that no one has wasted paper on
except an official report over Dutch cigars
years later they discuss the ruined museums houses the bricks the.

## Love in the Early Morning

There are days when the human body is a strange form,
when I lift the small delicate body of my 6-year-old
daughter laughing in the air above our great white
bed where you lie musing after coffee; her small dark
head gurgles with delight, your blonde hair falls over
your bare shoulders, your breasts have a drop of sweat.

The sunlight streams through the bright red curtains.
An old song rises from a car passing on the street outside.
My body is not delicate like hers or rich and female
like your own; my body is awkward flat and hard
distracted     without a job fame or money.
Our love is here in the family,
our fear and ambition are somewhere else
like a unicyclist coming down the 401.

## The Blue Sky

At first it was simply the blue sky.
We played under it, went fishing and threw stones.

I gave a talk in public school on flying saucers
and another talk on the components of the hydrogen bomb.

Then it became the blue sky of distances.

The world is irregular enough.
We don't want anything unusual to happen in the sky.

We want the sky to be blue and go on forever.

what we're talking about is atomic war what we're talking
about is atomic war disintegration red blasts mushroom clouds
nagasaki hiroshima test atolls enormous skin burns nevada flats
what we're talking about is atomic war the dead spread out over
the earth like white ants white worms what we're talking about
is insanity the insanity of governments trying to bluff each
other in a card game that doesn't have any money at the centre

We don't like to talk about it.

We like to think of the blue sky as an absolute parameter
the blue sky the blue sky as a frame that goes on forever.

We make love and watch television.

The problem will get solved by intellectuals who read Sagan.

We can only discover who our ancestors were,
what they did under a blue sky shaped like a woman's back,

By exploring the fields and cities of the earth.

I have terrible visions at times
of the earth being tossed up in the sky like a stone.

These are only visions. Meanwhile the earth is enormous.
It has blue oceans that are diverse with flowers and sponges.

The blue oceans have submarines that look like whales.

## New Age Confusions

**1**

A few hippies in overalls truck out of town
to go north and cultivate grains.
They can eat buckwheat and apples in winter.

I write in the morning and dream of Apollinaire
in the afternoon: a white-knuckled fool hooked
on the dichotomy between knowledge and art.

Lautrec fell from a horse on a country estate.
That was before the war and dadaism and Ubu Roi,
before de Gaulle's royal cavalcade through the

Arc de Triomphe,        . . . from Deux Magots this spring
the mind looks like a coloured photograph of a tree
whose roots become hands and feet.

**2**

Perhaps the Aquarians should settle in Peru.
The small farmers there have traditions and music.
At night they sit in a circle

At the foot of Macchu Picchu and exchange marvels,
like masters rapping out notes
on a soup bowl; they describe churches in the city

That lift up to the sky like great ribbed birds,
bazaars of cotton and exotic instruments,
circuses where acrobats perform impossible feats

And beautiful women gleaming with gold dust and sweat
dance naked on the backs of horses. The women sigh.
The bears pant with lust. The white-faced clowns do pratfalls

Until the circus closes and the audience departs by train.

**3**

Cottages are too general a solution;
I can spend an afternoon in the country
and watch the mating battles of moose.

I can vault the brass rails of the city,
compete for positions of power,
and be cut dead for the cut of my suit.

The store at the foot of my street
is a casual temptation. A quiet young guy
with big hands and three walls of boxes and tins.

Why don't I run for office as a dadaist mayor
or traffic in gold or buy an enormous beach?
Each day the dictionary falls open at a different page.

It is debatable if art is doing its job.

**4**

If it is true that the first agriculture
took place in Poland instead of Peking
I will have to revise my theories. New poems

And more complaints about the difficulties of life:
my heart crawling through another rat period
while my mind opens and closes like the maw of a fish.

Historical details are significant and so is love.
Logic and geography are essential. But meaning is abstract
and sometimes seems to look back at me through a telescope.

Rats have good eyes. I looked at Mars last night
and the landscape seemed as plain
as St. Marys where I was born—rubbled, easy to understand.

**5**

I talk to strangers who hand me newspapers,
bag ladies who believe that God lives
in the $9.95 transistor radio beside their bed,

Drunks who have never had a home in their lives,
executives who believe in modern technology,
conceptualists who want to make poems out of lake pebbles.

When I come home and undress,
Louise is sitting up in bed reading a history
of New York architecture. The windows are cool.

She opens her round arms like summer
and I put my head in her lap. She feeds me hambones.
I walk in circles until I relax.

**6**

The Civitas Dei isn't what I want
so much as a city with a diversity
and a pulse that brings things into focus.

I am like a wounded traveller. Travellers are clever.
Travellers are builders of towers and bridges. Design-
conscious guys with a rapport for basic materials.

I can watch the planets from Toronto or Denver
as easily as from the farm in rural Manitoba
or a fire at the foot of Machu Picchu.

Those murders out in the street are also a form of stars.

## Sweet Cotton

Diverse plant, *gutun*, useful for many things besides cloth:

Cotton oil for cattle feed, cotton waste for cleaning
machinery.

The early blues sequestered around this plant
uncultivated by Choctaw or Pawnee. Some early songs being work
tunes.

The word gin means to trap and also to begin.

Most of the blues I know are not about cotton.

A lot of blues are about giving her what she wants

About asking her to come downstairs in a red dress and
dance.

Diverse plant, *coton,* useful for many articles of clothing:

The American cigarette commercial a work of art.
Clean teeth and pale blue work shirts
with Lee and Levi's printed under the flap.

Torn dark jeans on soft-cocked straw-haired miners
stumbling home at 6 to collapse on bargain store cotton sheets.

Strong-seamed soft cotton loose around our bodies,
clinging in the subtle places under the arm as well as the crotch.

The sun is coming up and another week begins on the
calendar.

I am asking you to be kind and not to fray.

## The Black Pen

I hate to lose the pen I associate with my current work.
A different pen never seems quite the same.
The black pen has been mislaid. The black pen has been lost.
I wrote my last great idea with the black pen.
The black pen proved itself.
I want the black pen the plume noir and I want to rewrite
Champlain's dry journals.

Give me back the black pen.
The black pen knew what it was doing.
These other pens don't feel comfortable. Too fat. Too thin.
The black pen was technically superior to these other pens
and is probably lying right now in a pile of garbage
finding itself
balancing itself
centring
contemplating the eggshells grapefruit rinds and bits of toast.

## Family Reunion

Thank you, dear translator, for having been
and for singing still,
under the ground of a small town,

ironic hymns in Latin
and the occasional love poem
in archaic Greek,
singing
in the space between spaces,
dark nights like these,

while I am winter-locked
between my many selves,
my disarray,

singing
in the quiet void
where the pole turns;

and you turn also,
like a manx-tweeded falcon
around a widening star,

in touch with those before you
as I am with
you,

the flat-muscled pioneers from Glasgow,
hardy tavern owners from Bretony, phlegmatic Dutch clerks

fresh from the diked and tulip-
bordered flat lands
into a universe of forests and rivers;

thank my uncle Howard if you see him
turning in a slow spiral
                        of his own;

thank the goat tramp with athlete's
foot and string cufflinks
in his stolen shirts;

and the great aunt
who went insane
                        folding twenty-dollar bills in newspapers;

or your mother, Mary Cavers,
who painted that portrait of Beatrice
that hung in the livingroom for years;

thank all of them
                        in the broken earth-heart
of history, for having been,

images that become roots
while changes in the disturbed heart
alter perception and thought

against the dark night wind and brutal snow.

## Lakes

### 1

People who want to live beside the ocean are
fundamentalists.
The juxtaposition of land and sea makes a natural dyad.
Jane has a cottage at Musselman's Lake and Karen has a house
on Parkside Drive, bay-windowed, with a recording studio
in the renovated basement.
I visit Jane on Sundays, pushing the Ford van up Yonge Street
and turning east into the small townships that occur before
the land spreads steadily north, ploughed field after field
of what was unlimited and natural in the 19th-century
Scottish/English push from lake-front into the dry mouth
of colder weather.
The trees are yellow and orange and green the fields dark
brown with the last corn in crisp waves under the breeze.
This is the country I grew up in, a short region to the west,
St. Marys, Hamilton, Galt, small towns surrounded by fields,
and still remember as tangibly as a natural pattern.

We sit on two old lawn chairs on her front porch drinking
warm water and scotch while the sun falls slowly over the lake
and a fine line of sweat snails down our shoulders.
Brahms. Brahms.
Our knees bump like bass fiddles until we go inside for coffee.
She undoes the clumsy buttons on the plaid shirt after I kiss
her and stands quietly in front of me naked from the waist
in the dark light, her smile Dutch somehow, one hand busy
with the air, balancing it,
playing, then I am lost in her
our bodies fitting together like the lake and the rough stubble
along its edge. The clock ticks. Dogs bark outside.
Her underwear lying on top of my corduroy pants looks like

a surreal image of my connection to the country I grew up in
                                        and left foolishly
to waste my time in violence museum city,

of history, John Galt, Goldie's eventual millions, my grandfather
walking from Ayr to Galt once a month with a sack of flour,
of Jefferson and the separation of powers, of the lakes,
of Edison with a black tie, of silt drifting downstream
                                        in the clouded Potomac.

**2**

     But naturally I go back to my apartment in the city
with its general disorder, papers, books, junk, the day turns,
the nights are huge dark highways full of train wrecks
literature, love, sex, daily news, Dewar's, hangovers
                   and scrambled eggs.
I go out with Karen and feel at home in the city.
Karen is like a corn field with a bush of blueberries
at the heart, rehearsing a new performance piece in the middle
of her livingroom, morning sun leaf-strewn wild blonde hair,
plants, books, brass, a picture age 17 at highschool
                in Des Moines.
We make love on the green livingroom carpet and it almost
feels like the country. Who makes love out of doors anyway?
We get dressed and have a plain supper of bean sprouts,
yogurt, asparagus soup, apple betty, tuborg; we drink some scotch
             and I think
I am every adolescent boy in every novel from Sacramento
to White Horse and down again by train or imagination
continually choosing between different women
not even sure sometimes why I love them
as if they represent my ravished grandfather Duncan,
my lost aunts and uncles,
six-foot Hugh who parlayed a sack of flour into executiveship,
my dead father's medals and the clear steady hazel of his eyes
that burned out at you like the sun falling on slow poplars,
my mother's mother's great house in Washington where the boys
bet five-dollar gold pieces on which way the sun would shine,
or my father's wild mother lost in San Francisco with her bags
and her canvas bundle of brushes, burnt sienna, raw ochre,
               chromium yellow.
The pain of history is summarized by the way that simple
           geography
separates the powers of love and nostalgia, fern and brass,
past and present, until the general disorder of random city

requires more explanation, my disordered rooms, socks,
the dark elegant bar at the 22, my books, notes, the squared
calendar, wheat germ, eggs, the sermons of John Donne
                              with the bark
of the tough brown flea and the Puritan uprising behind them.

## 3

     I am the red and yellow and blue in that bundle of paints
against my will or otherwise
and lost in a history to which I am willing to be lost,
a farm boy intoxicated with a sense of distant events,
I understand this is a love of process not dissimilar
to the love of land that moves farmers in the early morning
to finish their coffee and walk to the barn still half asleep,
cows, chickens, pigs, bits of harness, plough points, wire.
I want to break backwards into my family history
and emerge with something more North American than flags
                                or bunting,
the Wilson brothers muttering in the steamy 5 a.m. barn,
the city turned around to face the Americas instead of the North,
some chicken feathers and tar for the fat mayor,
I want to put the different parts of our lives together,
the farms and the cities, the highways and the trains.
The dichotomies of North America confuse me.
Something happens to me with women that confuses me.
Ideas are simple.
Work is simple.
I associate Jane with the country and simplicity.
Karen with the city.
My desire for synthesis gets caught between highways.
Sometimes I think women are my connection with history.
My mother was my childhood geographer
and the men in my family were intellectuals and pragmatists.
Myself part both.
The city hums with all its different parts.
I walk west on Queen Street late at night
thinking about Galt and St. Marys and San Francisco.
The offices south of Queen are bright against the dark sky.

I turn up University walking slowly in the quiet
slight mist of the city after 12
two horse-drawn caleches for tourists
the city not completely asphalt
all these elements of the country still present
flickering in our consciousness like the flare of a gasoline match.

## Letter to the Mountains

Great One, give me a sign,
                          show me I am not alone
in nature:
              set the rose bush in the front yard on fire,
turn the stone red with flowers,
                                  split the dead stump
beside the house
                  with a burst of water.

All the elements I have balanced
                                  in the cool blue
light of the mind
                  have gone through transformation. Now they
are animals and the animals are set in motion.

Great One, you are an expert on consolidation.
Master of calendar stones and infinite cogs
that control the flux of days. Help me. I will enclose
boxes of footnotes documents and family records.

Use colour if the rose bush seems impossible.
Give some men black hats and others grey.

Turn the river white where it bends
                                    above the falls
where I used to fish when I was still a child
before I went into the world and lost my simple form.

That much may be enough:
                          I will use that
as an anchor
            and tell the rest
to heel like a yelping dog.

36

## Dream

I am standing in front of one of those long steel counters
at a seedy hotel concession waiting for something to eat.
The fat man behind the counter gives me a bowl of soup.
I take a slice of bread and begin to break off bits.
"Hey," the fat man yells, "you're taking too much of that."
I tell him my hands are clean and show him my hands.
"That's not the point," he says, "you're taking too much."
I put back most of the bread and walk over to a cutlery box.
A ragged man passes behind me and I pick up a pair of scissors.
Something for defence. Silence. And pass into the loud room.

## Wrecked Boats

The massive ship goes over on its side within days of
$\qquad\qquad\qquad\qquad\qquad$ the New England coast.
Life boats are unhooked from their couplings.
Dark morning, no gulls, hysteria is present everywhere.
Fear predominates and is balanced with violent arguments.
The Irish sailors are calmer wider-shouldered with dark
sweaters under their wool jackets. Several women
have begun praying and the chaplain moves in to lead them.
The Irish sailors take nine of the life boats and pray
a little differently.

      Hayle Mary full of grayce, The Lord is with thee,
      blessed art thou amongst women. Blessed is the fruit
      of thy womb, Jaysus. Hohly Mary mather of God,
      pray for us poor sinners now and at the hour
      of our dayth.

The day is beginning to clear. The Irish sailors put
themselves into the oars. Real land will appear.
They have a different view of things than the rest
of the travellers. They believe that St. Patrick swam
to Ireland from some other country. They are at home
with the idea of water and darkness and God.
The Atlantic is cold and the sun has not come out. The
Irish sailors are rowing to Ireland.

## a short history of scottish acumen in the region of galt

got up before the sun and worked all day like dray horses
dripping with sweat until the dim fields were ploughed brown
back to the stone cabin for tea and a cold wash at the door
larger than english and solid thick-shouldered earthy
barley a thick soup millet slabs of bread potatoes corn
children closing their books for a game on the cold floor
month-old newspapers      a new buckle for a piece of harness
passages from first corinthians      passages from isaiah
the coming of wheat banks corn banks and angus cattle banks
macdougal down at the arms buying drinks for the bar room
the woman finished mending shirts socks a dress last to bed
in the straw loft upstairs smelling of oatcakes and camphor
quiet, she says to him, you're drunk, the children are awake
ah well, she says, they're asleep, slow spin settling calm
green trees that go on forever without defining a district
one friend a pharmacist with his own store south of detroit
a cousin's death in glasgow, doctor saw, broken harnesses
a thousand blue-eyed Cavers marching from preston to york
mad bulls lowing      the coming and passage of slow winter
of banks seed insurance farm equipment more stone buildings
president now with a large office and a view of the grand river
the brass works the knife foundry      perplexed by mortgage

## Rutabagas

The first step to be taken on the rutabaga market is simple.

Buy up all the cheap rutabaga producers and sit on them.

Then introduce fresh rutabagas at $2.00 a pound.
Run some large magazine spreads on rutabagas.
Rutabagas contain natural vitamin C.
Talk about their history.
Talk about famous people who have enjoyed them.

Gradually drop the price to $1.50 a pound.

"Rutabagas become popular." Begin to market them seriously.

Run spreads of different recipes for rutabagas.
A special section for vegetarians.
A special section for roast beef diners.
A special section for small bistros that cook with woks.

This is the way to make people happy.
This is the way to enjoy life and make money.

Soon almost everyone will take rutabagas for granted.
Fabulous.
Now raise the price of rutabagas very slowly to $2.75 a pound.

Amazing. Two years ago they'd never heard of rutabagas.
Now they're in love with turnip and want nothing else.

Great.

Who knows what rutabagas are? They want them.

Maybe a new rutabaga can be introduced. A lighter rutabaga.
A more chemically attuned rutabaga for $3.45 a pound.

Great. Everyone is happy and they go to the market.

I am some distance away in all this. Removed.
I sit in my office and read the newspapers. I smoke cigars.

When rutabagas go to $3.75 a pound I cannot contain myself.
I throw my newspapers in the garbage and make love to my
                              secretary
with the day's correspondence falling all over the floor.

I am a success. I am the rutabaga king of North America.
I am so excited I can hardly do up my pants.
A pale frightened man with a cigar and a back problem.
I go down in the elevator glowing with pride.

Rutabagas. I can't stand them. They taste like musty potatoes.

The very thought of them makes me sick to my stomach.

I vomit in an ashcan and go home and listen to Brahms
smoke some dope      have some dinner      look out at the night
write a slow poem about the formal structure of glass.

## The Night

The night is streets that extend for blocks of neon and shadow.
The street ends where the neon ends in pure darkness.
It could be the end of the city or the end of the night
or where the police are parked or where a dealer is waiting.
The end of any one of these streets is a parameter.
Taxis ply up and down the street with their windows down
taking a drunk home a late shopper a couple after dinner,
a geek who has just gotten out of Kingston for bad cheques,
a woman who has just had a fight with her husband.
Norman le Coeur stops outside the all-night diner for a hot dog
and looks across at the pin-ball emporium where the young
prostitutes are standing around in cut-off shorts.
A sad schmuck plainclothesman lounges against the front
                                of a store
la douleur des nuits de la rue Yonge     la douleur de la dark
Bobby Fedora comes past and snaps open tomorrow's racing form
the horses line up at the gate behind the huge window
of a furniture store and charge west along Dundas Street.
Parker comes by and plants his enormous bulk against a meter.
The bars are closed and the street slides into its sad sweet
night life coming down and waking up and cruising.
The hawks cruise targets and the doves cruise falcons.
Die Nacht ist in ourselves and reaches out to the night like lovers
shifting between the sheets of a new hotel and tumbling into sex.
The only girl I've seen wearing a red dress this week
curves her pink tongue at me from the back of a Metro cab.
She smiles like a dark angel and I walk over to her out of
boredom out of excitement out of interest in the car.
How do I know that she doesn't have syphilis?
We're both clean.

"You remember me," she says, "Jackie, from Marvin's place."
She lights a joint in the back seat while the paranoid driver

42

tells us he's being watched by agents from outer space.
The grass is pungent. We drive east then north on Mount
Pleasant past the cemetery where the dead people sleep
past the dark restaurants and traffic lights and art stores.
We stop outside a white building that looks circa 1970.
Jackie gives el driver a sawbuck and we walk into the light
of a foyer with some pleasant kitsch deco art.
She looks more innocent than a teacher.
La notte is full of contradictions.
We ascend on the back of the dark elevator shaft
like an angel with the skirt of her red dress around our hips.
"No money," I tell her, "no francs no marks no lira."
She pours two drinks at a small bar while I put some music on
and then in the bedroom she undresses like a young stripper
doing it just for laughter and music
and then night again      la notte sounds more like morning,
cool pungent sounds of Ella Fitzgerald from the livingroom
and one more scotch and ice while Jackie lies stretched
on the large bed arching her perfect hips and kneading
a muscle in the small of her back      the red dress folded
over the back of an antique chair and the lights of all the
great buildings to the south flickering like pale gold dominoes
the occasional car wheeling past and the quiet plaintive sounds
of early sparrows as I lie down beside her perfect body
and drift to sleep.

## The Distance

After you've sobered up for the afternoon & watered
the dry geraniums & made fresh coffee the distance
comes like a large flower breaking open inside your head.
The distance comes like a gift.
Frozen butter sunlight on highrise tower widows.
The distance comes like an ice-cube breaking inside your heart.
The world fades.
The horns fade & the dust fades & your mother fades.
Genteel bruised guilty & softly accusative.
The pockets of rust & grease & broken auto parts fade
until there is nothing left in the mind
except brown water & trout.
We are made of natural things & disagree from error.
The woman comes out of the broken ice-cube with her mouth
like a red leaf & her hands cupping her full breasts
like white afternoon bricks cupping beds of flowers.
I think I'm going to kill someone this afternoon.
I'm going to kill the first man I see who uses the word paki.
I'm going to kill the first man I see who does a hit & run
                              on a small child.
I'm going to blow the sombitch apart like strawberry jam.
The distance comes like a vertebra fitting back into place.
Not distance from the woman with blue flowers in her mouth
but distance from arguments that don't make sense.
Violence satisfies frustration.
Not new poems or a clean apartment or some new books.
Not fifty dollars or some new music or a good fuck.
Not distance from the typewriter or people you love
but distance from the old knot the old angst the old fucked-up
pork-chop bone & indecision of fear & careful poker hands
& being completely sure of your ideas
although ideas are never something to be completely sure of.
Distance from the old failure of confidence.
From the kid lying in the snow with blood on his mouth

44

after you hit him too hard with your skates.
From the fear of losing & not being able to replenish.
Distance from the old knot.
The guy's face screaming at you eyes crazy mouth flecked
with spit broken ear dope wreck veins in hands bulging.
Distance from the phlegm spasm in the blood of the throat.
The ice-cube lodged in the heart.
The '57 Chev that wouldn't start until I kicked it for half
an hour until my boots were wrecked dead drunk 17 in a
parking lot off the 401 yelling at the smudge-rivered April moon.
Distance from the dead father un-read Juvenal & bad trumpets.
From the duplicity of yellow winter morning kitchens & the great
lie of snap-beans love & natural faith.

## Stepfathers

There you were again in my dream last night,
burly, caught in mid-step, crop-headed or bald,
old parka splashed with chicken blood,
carrying a shotgun
or was that a blur of shadow I saw?

I followed you into the corridor
of a huge building but you disappeared.

I walked into the spotless public john
to wash my hands and you appeared in the doorway.

I had this incredible feeling of strength;
the .38 on my right hip kicked like a mule.

Old man, you die but you live around.

Pig mouth is pig mouth. Nothing touched clean.

Mercy is baffling. Adjustment blurs meaning.

My final image in the dream is always
the way you slide down the wall
blood all over the tiles, clutching at nothing.

The blood on my hands sickens me.

I want to give up my concept of family honour.

I want to save you.

## The True Story of Pat Garrett

Pat Garrett was a moustached cow-brain and a follower
but biographies and feature films need characters
that can be built up to create a balance of tension.

What actually happened was nothing.

Garrett rode around in circles talking to his horse.
There wasn't any drama except for the tumbleweed.
No one had a clear idea of where Billy was staying.
Garrett went to the Maxwell ranch by accident.
Suddenly there he was on Pete's ranch in the middle of the night
with Billy walking oblivious along the wooden porch
coming back from the meat shed.
Garrett didn't even sneak up behind the Kid standing at a window.
Garrett was surprised by him.
He shot the Kid from the darkness of Pete Maxwell's bedroom
when Billy walked in framed by the moon.
Why make a toad into a model of intelligence?
He would have probably missed in normal sunlight.
Birds fly like stones.
Garrett was an oil-slick on the great highway of Billy's life.

The Kid was reckless by nature.
He had no desire to go to South America anyway.
Peru doesn't exist. Neither does Egypt.
He wanted to stay in the southwest forever.
The moon came out like a huge yellow New Mexico flower.
Billy turned to the voice in the moonlight and slipped and fell.

## Mars

I don't think about God very much
these days but
                    I think about Mars a lot,

          concentrating on the topography
and subtle shadings
                    a 19-minute radio-beam
away from the green earth;

          how it would feel to walk
in that kind of weightlessness
first thing in the morning;
                              is it really
one in six or is it one in four?

          God is in space perhaps,
there may be various gods in space,
but mainly I think about Mars,

          knowing I am dry with a peculiar thirst
which can be slaked only
                         by photographs
of the broad desert, the possibly verdant forests
and the stone memories fragmented
beside craters;
                    wanting to know
was it always a desert,
                              who/what broke those craters open
and turned the probable rivers underground?

**Rustic**

You put the loaf of bread in the oven and let it bake.
It comes out golden brown with a light crust
not like that of an orange or a birch log
but more like that of a potato or the fine chaff of grain.
What would bread be like if it didn't have a crust?
The crisp nourishing inside would have to be different.
It wouldn't keep properly even wrapped in cool leaves.
People would have trouble all over the country.
The bread would go stale overnight and leave them starving.
They make bread differently in the Middle East. No crust.
Give them some water and they'll make unleavened bread
while they trek. Their history is a history of oases.

# The Canadian Prairies View of Literature

First of all it has to be anecdotal; ideas don't exist;
themes struggle dimly out of accrued material like the shadow
of a slow caterpillar struggling out of a large cocoon;
even this image itself is somewhat urban and suggests
the tree-bordered streets of small southern Ontario towns.
Ontario towns are eastern; French towns are European;
the action should take place on a farm between April
                                  and cool October;
nature is quiet during winter, it snows and there's a lot of it,
the poem blazes in the schoolteacher's head like an image
of being somewhere else like Rome or Costa Rica;
the novel shifts in the articulate reporter's head
and surveys the relationships between different farms.
Sometimes the action happens in the beverage rooms and cheap
hotels area of a small town that has boomed into a new city;
Indians and Métis appear in the novel wearing the marks
of their alienation like a sullen confusion of the weather;
a woman gets married and another woman has a child;
the child is not old enough to plough a field and therefore
does not become a focus of interest except as another mouth.
They sit around with corn shucks in their head and wonder
who they should vote for, the question puzzles them,
vote for the one with the cracked shoes, he's a good boy,
or the one who jumped over six barrels at a local dance;
their regionalism is like a nationalism of the land;
the small farmers struggle against equipment dealers;
their wives struggle against patriarchal cowshit;
their intellectuals dislike the east which gives them form
allowing their musings and discontents to flower into rancour.

Afternoon light, aged 12, I walk down the small side
streets of Galt, past South Water, musing and rancorous, adrift,
not quite like Rimbaud leaving Charleville for Paris,
my hands in my windbreaker pockets like white stones,
and promise myself once again that when I get to the city

everything will happen, I will learn all of its history
and become the best writer they have ever dreamed of.
I'll make them laugh and sometimes make them cry,
I'll drink their whisky and make love to all their wives,
the words tumbling out of my mouth as articulate as
                                    the young Hector,
the corn under my shirt awkward a little rough light brown dry
and making me itch at times.

## Dostoievski Discovers the Novel

Let us take *The Red and the Black* by the inimitable Stendhal
and lay it on the table of a livingroom in 19th-century Russia.

A young man comes downstairs for breakfast and finds the book;
he sits drinking tea and reads through the first chapter.

The moody Russian sunlight shifts outside the large windows;
he forgets about breakfast and sits scratching his short beard.

Napoleon marched all the way to Moscow but forgot about
                                                    winter;
this book explains some of the other things Napoleon forgot.

The young man continues drinking tea over another chapter and
the book turns into a yellow flower moving around in his heart.

The proud bruised mind drifts down and sniffs the flower
like a dog taking hold of a partridge out in the Russian woods.

The flower breaks up into grain and becomes an enormous field;
the young man's body turns into earth and his head nods like
                                        a railway.

St. Petersburg is like the Paris of eastern Europe
a great city put together with boards and stones,

Blocked by the Balkans and by a stupid war with Poland,
the Poles should have won, the best cavalry officers in Europe;

Blocked by the Germans who went to school on St. Petersburg,
their ale houses their bleak army their bitter sausages.

The flower turns orange to gold and then dark fiery yellow
like a huge grain sunflower in the shape of a fist by Van Gogh.

Van Gogh walks across the small grey stone bridge at Arles
and holds out his paintbrush spattering the young man's shirt.

The huge yellow fist rages against the limitations of the bored
Russian students who are tired of folk music and La Fontaine;

They are a long way from the great oceans of the world,
blocked from the east and have never heard of Pennsylvania.

The young man continues the novel and makes copious notes;
Dostoievski has discovered Stendhal and a concept of Aloysha.

## All the Beautiful Young Men

Slowly I come down to the hardwood floor of the apartment
floating back into myself, picking up poems and familiar objects.

Alcohol leads to grass and cocaine leads to anarchy.

I change into a corduroy jacket and jeans
and go for a walk along Bloor Street.

The men I find most attractive are always young, pragmatic
broad-shouldered and just a little pretentious.

That pretentiousness, I think, is like the flattened ninth
in a good blues.
                    Even Beethoven wears thin
after your body cannot accept any more intelligence.

## South American Sailors

South American sailors are religious and wear gold earrings.
They love music and like to sit around in small groups
singing old songs they remember from the cities and villages.
The ocean is completely different from the jungle,
older and yet it looks new, there are no trees and no macaws.
Some of the sailors like to feed scraps of food to the gulls.
Occasionally the sailors see whales.
Sometimes they see other ships.
At night on late watch they take the cleanest-shaven
most beautiful young sailor, Juan, who comes from the Andes,
and dress him in a black shirt and a red scarf.
Crazy Juan whirls and glides around the deck of the ship
snapping his fingers like castanets while the sailors clap
and the fish coast under the surface of the blue water.
The ship is carrying coffee and Argentine beef.
There are no horses on board but some of the men have journals.
Day breaks and reflects in the water like a long blue dream.
Juan collapses exhausted.
The tango is a complex form which does not appear in English.
The sailors pick up their tobacco
and carry Juan downstairs to his bunk before breakfast.

## The Way Artists Live

With one hand in their wallet and the other on a new title.
Desperately.
From seriousness and despair to manic exuberance.
In abandoned lofts or semi-furnished bed-livingrooms
    or lowrise apartments with Picasso prints.
With the poem as a white shape in the middle of the night.
With the new painting as a faded red barn.
With a choreography of horses.
With an awkwardness about their role in the world
    since they are neither carpenters or mathematicians.
On eggs and liquor and bread and whatever else.
Standing in the middle of moors with enormous longbows
    aimed at the hearts of critics.
Wearing the same clothes for 10 days at a time in the belief
    that to change them would alter the centre of perception.
With partners fundamentally opposed to the nature of art.
Staggering home drunk from bars where they have spent
    the evening trying to convince a plaster statue
    that Da Vinci was actually a woman.
In trees armed with a quantity of stones for throwing
    at cousins daughters brothers psychiatrists and dwarf nuns.
In black suits with rusty black hats and forelocks.
With an abundance of books describing the nature of history.
In raincoats with rusty black hats and Smith & Wesson .45s.

At the centre of new events looking at their point of origin.
At the centre of their own language.
On chickens fish leeks spinach and marrowbone soup.
With the obvious conviction that all relationships should
    begin with red wine a sexual act and a partridge.
With an increasing tendency to prefer partners of the same
    sex unless general agreement on feminism is possible.
With a constant belief in the transcendence of commerce.
Beside themselves.

Camped in small northern towns waiting for helicopters.
Standing with their mothers.
With a copy of Montaigne in the kitchen.
With copies of *Elle* in the bathroom.
With copies of Althusser in the hallway.
In front of themselves.
Prepared at all times to defend the city of their birth
    from invasion by enemy troops martian robots or the treasury.
With penguins racoons geckos armadillos and dalmatians.
With 2 x 4s to beat landlords.
At the centre of deserts blasting the rocks for water.
With dogs horses pigs cows and moose.
Within walking distance of bodies of water capable of
    fundamental trade and commerce.
On the flatbeds of railway cars writing or painting with quarts
    of Bushmill's under a large black umbrella.

# Men Suspected of Faggotry

All men who prefer philosophy to conversation or sports
men who prefer cooking to industrial arts
men who are disinclined to punch out rivals
men who listen to Puccini on Sunday mornings
men who wear black cotton underwear
men who turn up the collar of their shirt
men who work at office jobs and play squash in the evening
men who wear heavy stone or metal cuff-links
men who buy ensembles to go jogging
men who have more than one mirror in the bathroom
all men who wear two different colognes
men who are interested in bathrooms
men who accept a division of household tasks
men who resent or are not respectful to their mothers
men who are sloppy
men who succumb to self-pity
men who don't pay their debts
men who prefer fashion shows to pornography
men who are writers or painters
men who aren't interested in the history of mining
men who wear baseball jackets
men who dream about Peru
men who smoke cigars
men who are self-conscious about putting their arm
                              around another man's shoulder
men who allow their wives to make basic decisions
men who are faithful to their wives
men who are married
men who are unfaithful to their wives with other men or with
                              women who resemble their mothers
men who have never served in the Canadian infantry

men who don't know how to ride a horse
men who like to be photographed riding horses or bicycles
men who are interested in snakes
men who are afraid of snakes
men who have sex with sheep or other animals
men who study photographs of themselves
men who are put off by a woman brushing her teeth in the
                                    morning
men who wear dresses
men who wear a large number of rings
men who find this poem embarrassing
men who find this poem hilarious
men who are afraid of failure and drink too much
men who are self-conscious about another man's cock in the
                                    club shower
men who are bored with success
men who miss their fathers at odd times of the day
men who don't know how to put up a house
men who are not self-sufficient
men who have no projects of general significance
both sexes who practise affectation
all postmen who ring twice without an answer
dogs of either sex who fuck furniture legs
men who prefer religion to having a drink
men who envy other men       men who are afraid of authority
men who are in prison

## The Power of Uniforms

It doesn't matter how many dark mysterious rotting-away
rooming-houses the police walk into
sometimes at 3 in the morning holsters loosened
or how many bar-room brawls they break up
cars stopped on dark sideroads, midnight hi-jacks
or how many desperate bank-robbers
they pursue into the lofts of dark country barns

the power of uniforms is amazing      almost as if
a naked man or woman lacks clear social meaning

every now and then a police constable gets shot in the head
or falls off a motorcycle on an icy road

but how often do you hear about one of them
being stabbed seventeen times in the face and body
being blown up on a plane en route to Acapulco
being electrocuted with a toaster tossed in the bath
being blown up with dynamite under their pillow
being raped by five men and then bludgeoned to death?

The power of uniforms is amazing      almost as if
the uniform corresponds to an electronic code
a monitor or electrode in the assailant's head

The worst minds in the country respect the police
and reserve their most violent emotion for each other.

The gun and the buttons are important.
You can see the 17-year-old boys lining up
in front of the police posters and nodding their heads,
appraising the way the uniform fits
oblong with neat shoulders and black leather straps;

the gun and the size of the average constable are important
but the uniform itself has a precise social logic
suggesting precincts and squad cars and radios,
other men wearing the same clothing,
suggesting a recognition of these facts
by storekeepers and housewives, bouncers and taxi drivers.

The uniform has a light of its own.
The man carries it like a circus performer carrying a ball.
The uniform walks by itself and talks over the short-wave radio.

Order is everything. The shift breaks and the men hang
their uniforms up sadly and drive home
naked in windbreakers and grey flannel slacks.

## West End Livingroom at Night

Some evenings there's nothing more beautiful in the world
than a nude mannequin with a black velvet tie
looking back at you in the half-lit room while you drink
your scotch and listen to the cold rain outside.
An obscure 17th-century Polish composer
talks about sadness with a violin and two pianos.
The mannequin is as white as chalk or marble.
The expression on her face is serene and suits the angle
of her naked breasts. You pour another drink
and put a grey felt slouch fedora on her head. Night.

Somewhere in Poland they are getting up to go to work.
Someone is talking about a film he'd like to make.
The number of odd things collected in this livingroom
is so extensive that you're running out of room for books.

The livingroom is warm: ceramics, a crib, an old Coca-Cola
sign, a bicycle, a Picasso print, a small red tree.
You think of the walnuts scattered on the front lawn
for the landlord's children to collect. Car wheels whirr
outside. She parts her mouth and winks with one reflective
                              dark blue eye.

## Trains

What does it matter if I think of other people sometimes
when we make love? What difference does it make if another
woman, a tiger, a man we saw on the train to Albany, walks
across the landscape of my mind while you move your hips
under me with those incredible leaps of desire?
You are the white field fundamental to all these things.
You are the bridge which supports them
even as you support me.
                              I carry you half-naked
into the bedroom and your hips lift me above the falling day.
I come down from a great height and enter you again.
The woman's hair is reddish. The man on the train laughs but
with amazement      and the quality of your mercy is intact.

## How a Writer Should Explore the Nature of Fashion

Buy an expensive leather shoulder bag but don't wear it.
Patronize a good cheap restaurant once a month.
Do not walk around with a knapsack.
Be clean-shaven so you can show up occasionally with a stubble.
Read fashion magazines.
Find out what people are interested in.
Correct your grammar.
Learn how to ask for the washroom in Belgian.
Respect people who know more than you do.
Study the miraculous photographs of Eugène Atget.
Read a lot of history.
Don't let other writers rush past you with flashy moves.
Circulate rumours that you're becoming a Catholic.
Consider ex-communicating the Pope.
Get your hair cut regularly. Wear white in the summer.

Live in a seedy downtown apartment.
Walk through the garbage of alleyways at night.
Learn the streets of the city by heart.
Read the newspaper every day.
Go to the opera at least once.
Write at least 10 great poems.
Don't let interviewers get between you and the audience.

God expects you to produce a number of poems about opposites.
Hope John Cale records one of your songs.
Don't write for yourself but write for people like yourself.
Don't be afraid of fashion or the word will devour you.
Don't be afraid of the word popular.
These are reasonable words for different things.
Oranges are popular and oranges are beautiful.
Think about the way people understand things.
Think about highway signs.
Highway signs are a form of fashion.

So are highways.
Don't use drugs. Drugs are bad for your mind.
Invent some fashions of your own.
Invent something useful.
The world can be saved by a series of deliberate steps.
The children can be saved and the whales can be saved.
Remember that nothing is perfect.
Do not accept the rationale for seaweed diets.
Talk less and think more.
Consider the idea that less is more.
Do not apply this idea to wages.
Remember that nothing is perfect.
Work out regularly. Be positive. Wear white in the summer.
Learn how to write. Believe in love.

## Nobody Knows Anything About Art Anymore

Hans Hofmann was a terrific guy.
Hofmann was all about a perception of the body as organic
even when viewed from various disparate positions;
Hofmann was a post-cubist     he goes back to the demoiselles
as Picasso goes back to Cézanne who was dull but suggestive
beautiful old man     quiet eyes     grey beard     blue shirt
sitting calmly in front of his canvas out in the country.
I wanted to be a painter once     I wanted to paint apples
girls reclined in armchairs     posters of starchy policemen
abandoned farms     a downtown crowd     a loaf of bread.
Goya used oils when someone at court wanted their picture,
the Maja bores me but the monster's etchings are fantastic:
dark smudged bitter light photographs of the unconscious country.
I wanted to be a painter once:     I practised drawing horses
nude women with fantastic red hats     waiters with broken
                              noses
I gave it all up     you can either draw or you can't; how do
abstract painters do it? It's bewildering but I figured it out.

They sit up all night with their blah paintings spread on the
floor and ride back and forth over them with rusty bicycles
they have children who come and pour buckets of green and white
paint over their mistakes     the crooked shoulder     the knee
that doesn't look like a knee     the head too large for its body,
Lautrec would have loved the head too large for its body;
they hang their painting out on fire-escapes and let pigeons
crap on them     city smoke accumulates     flying bricks
they bring them back into the studio and burn them with cigars;
the result has meaning because it's a formal record–
of cigars     of implements     of destroyed canvas
and is therefore about something after all:     about the vacancy
of their lives     about their lack of belief in form     their
idiocy     their vapid media-ism     their inward deception
their failure to understand colour     their blindness to light

66

## For Joan Miró on His 85th Birthday


Born in 1893, in Catalonia, province of sunny skies and cool
                              brown earth,
12 years after Picasso,
                    master of yellow flowers and bizarre
                    red birds,
what can you tell us about the blue skies over Spain,
the students sitting around in the cafés of Paris,
the death of Lorca,
                 the exile of Buñuel
or the farouche master's new film—*That Obscure Object of Desire*?

What can you say except that Paris was an age of masters
who wrote and painted under sunnier skies than our own.

You are one of the great flowers, one of the great wry birds,
that leap from the human heart
                              like dark speech from the throat
of a young man startled suddenly on a trestle bridge by a horse.

We have the sun and the earth, our mathematics and a good cellar,
but you are a part of the light itself; even the ink-stains on the
print-table in your atelier are inhabited by the birds of the air.

A blind man sees nothing, muses, like the incredible Borges,
or plays hot funk piano with the exuberance of Ray Charles.

Strike us, master, we are the brilliant young men of the grey city,

leave us restless with yellow flowers caught in our shirts
your great birds swooping down to perch on our heads like
                              statues.

# American Buffalo Nickels

## American Buffalo Nickels

I put the coin flat on the desk looking out over New York
my first time in the city staying at the Algonquin Hotel
thinking of the wagons sent west for farms      for gold
my grandfather bound for California in 1896 brought back
stories a gold belt buckle ingots and a black journal;
how is it possible for history to come alive after it's dead?
Not possible at all      but the light's strange in this room,
the buffalo has his head lowered      big curved horns
the folded eyes look as cruel as winter
and suggest the Sioux in their winter camps out on the plains.
Obviously I think too much      an obsessive intellectual,
an emotional writer who goes wild on cheap rye,
but somebody should help me      who can I phone at this hour?
Every one of us loves money and is willing to sell his brother
but nobody wants to be gored by a huge buffalo
or left helpless out on the frozen prairies in winter.
Dim light      smoky mirror      nothing left to drink
this sonofabitch has his big head down like history
and is obviously about to charge

## The Coming Of Black To North America

The Puritans brought black to Boston and Salem
They liked the opposites of black and white together
Dunked witches who were shown wearing black only
Wanted their wives to wear modest grey
Brother Wilson      Sister Taylor
White tablecloths for the Lord's bountiful food
Turkeys squash yams stringbeans corn apple pies alderberry
The Presbyterians brought grey and brown to Toronto and Galt
They extrapolated a range of muted homespun shades
Built spired stone churches at a distance from their houses
The Presbyterians didn't believe in witches
but every street had a person who was supposed to be crazy
The Puritans didn't shoot buffalo or trap beaver
but they were tough on malefactors      stocks and the press
Their children became drunkards and inventors and ministers
Edwards saw spiders marching along the branch of a tree
Their influence is everywhere in the concept of productivity
There was almost no black in their lives whatsoever
except for their clothing and the concept of sin
The Presbyterians liked oatmeal and scotch whisky
John Galt saw neat grey factories rising out of the quarries
The radical socialists were wiped out by the English banks
Their influence is everywhere in the concept of propriety
chickens squash peas stringbeans corn apple pies alderberry
Their children became journalists and social workers and poets

The great black of the New World inspires me
the black of coal      coal dust      the great mines of Springhill
and Harlan County      the black stone of Butte      the black
under northern birchbark      the black oil struck by northern

workers in Petrolia     the black tongues of imported chows
the black of rotten avocados on ships in Vancouver     the
black creosote ties of railways     the black hats of western
                              gunmen
the black skin of African men and women     jostled on Dutch ships
from the Gold Coast to Charlestown     north after Lincoln to
Nova Scotia and Seaforth     the black of trees     maples poplar
elm willow in white winter     the grey stone of churches
the grey of grey flannel suits     the black of black iron pans
black underwear nylons socks garters wallets and purses
Minneapolis matrons in black taffeta     actor waiters in black
bow ties     Italian bricklayers in black suits at the funeral of
Sacco and Vanzetti     the black glass fake mirrors of 5th Avenue
restaurants     the black wallets of King Street     the black hood
in the demonstration after the death of Emanuel Jaques     the
black limousines outside the Sheraton Hotel for the IMF conference
the black tuxedos of Bay Street brokers and lawyers
reading the *Financial Times* in the middle of a formal ball

The Puritans were congregational extremists.
The Presbyterians explored the nature of conscience,
None of them understood how primary colours dance, poise, lunge
                              out of
black earth clear water and sing.
There was almost no black in their lives whatsoever
except for their tongues and the dark Lake Ontario night.

## Traffic

All over North America, the roads are designed
like coloured drawings on a map; looked at without
the names, it could be a drawing of our mind.

It is the mind of North America and the traffic
moving along the different angles of the mind
is our lives; it is everyone going to work
and coming home in the evening; it is the sales reps
of the major corporations making calls on clients;
it is a young couple going for a picnic in the country
or a sad artist driving out to the farm
to do a perfect sketch of an old man's barn; it is
employment for almost 23% of the population;
it is work and happiness and everyone has accidents
as they flow along the mind of North America.

These are examples from a few of these accidents;

> Coming home, I drove into the wrong
> house and collided with a tree I don't have.

That was a salesman coming home from his boss's party.

> I pulled away from the side of the road,
> glanced at my mother-in-law
> and headed over the embankment.

That was a middle-aged accountant who has always
dreaded his family.

> An invisible car came out of nowhere,
> struck my vehicle and vanished.

That was a visiting Cambridge mathematics professor.

The pedestrian had no idea which direction to go,
so I ran over him.

North America is wonderful. For the price of a car
it makes all of us into aristocrats. The pedestrian
was fortunate that he wasn't pulling a donkey.

I told the police that I was not injured, but on
removing my hat, I found that I had a fractured skull.

That was a trucker who understands America. He will
continue driving day and night because he loves driving.

The last quote must be a young man schooled in the works
of Li Po. It is Li Po's message for America:

I was thrown from my car as it left the road. I was
later found in a ditch by some stray cows.

*Examples taken from an Avis publication*

## Sandwiches

A woman went into the same restaurant every Tuesday night
for a month and asked the counterman for a toasted
ham sandwich on brown with a chocolate milkshake.

"Make the milkshake really creamy," she asked him,

"and the sandwich should be crisp but not over-toasted."

Every night the counterman told her the same prices
and said he'd be glad to make them up but the woman would
shake her head and refuse to pay.

The second Tuesday night the woman went in and ripped her dress.

"Give me the toasted ham sandwich and the chocolate
                                milkshake,"

she said, shaking the extravagant menu in his face.

The third Tuesday night the woman went in and posed like an
angel in front of the blue and purple Wurlitzer.

The counterman was unimpressed by this and showed her the menu.

The fourth Tuesday night the woman went in with handfuls of mud.

"Give me the toasted ham sandwich and the chocolate milkshake,
you male chauvinist sonofabitch," she said, "I'm starving."

So the counterman sat down with her and lit her cigarette
and said, "OK, rip the dress, pose, handfuls of mud, but tell me
what have you got against paying for it, against using money?"

"Money," the woman said, "money's shit, I hate money,

"Macdonald and George Washington staring at you with those big
doleful spaniel eyes of theirs. Give me the toasted ham sandwich,

"you bastard,
and the chocolate milkshake because you love me."

## Geese

For John Ashbery          *Nobody knows the etymology of the word*
                              *anarchy.*   Paul Morain


Pelicans don't walk so much as they run or actually stagger.
Ostriches are cretinous.
But geese are like anarchists.
The Greeks being in love with sheep had little to say of birds
but geese, maligned as the common goose, white with yellow bill,
geese, from the German *goosse* or *gosse* for gosling,
are superior to other birds on land water in air,
head cocked in the Balzac light, eyes peeled to pick up the
                              brown landscape.
Hitler wasn't a goose so much as a fetid ugly duckling
imploring the bruised and unemployed to identify with treason.
Some weisenheimer invented the term goose-step to describe
the eagerness with which farm boys tried to outdo each other
marching to ruin while the ugly duckling sulked over
                              mineral water.
One more misnomer added to the dark and ribald farm list,
goose, a foolish goose, to goose someone, a Christmas goose;
the Jews light candles at Chanukah and eat chopped liver,
leavened bread, spices and oil, soup, pike and carp;
a goose is harder to catch and hold in the farmyard than duck
larger and smarter than chicken      who eats nighthawks?
Goose      large and intelligent with a gift for invective and whim
denied water and air      master of dry brown farmyard earth,
maligned always for the surreal way it cocks its long head;
goose      bequeather of soft feathers      all the great goose-
                              feather-
comforted brass beds of country inns where you fuck till sunrise;


78

goose gatz gazpacho gadget      geese wild in the corn fields.
The greatness of goose is arrogance without cunning or malice,
prized for their livers      the jubilant goose livers of Strasbourg,
half a loaf of fresh bread and a pitcher of ice-cold beer;
red wine and white sheets the first night she undoes
                                    the blue dress,
the fields stretching outside like a yellow dream of fortune—
but goose is triumphant      eyes crested with grain,
and burns down its master's barn when the gates are open.
Goose      maligned littérateur and midnight rambler
the sharp eyes and the great wings      its heart abstract
the rich liver to be eaten for courage      before the strawberries
                                    and milk of je ne sais quoi.

## White Rats

*For Michael Ondaatje*


    Perhaps there is nothing more beautiful
for the sad reflective man
                              than to watch these rats
solve puzzles.

Their balance is perfect.
Each whole body tumbles forward twitching nose
and delicate paws like a flash of weather.
A wire cage and a slice of tomato.
They use their intense but limited neural faculties
to solve problems that represent our own.
Diagrams are diagrams.
Their minds are like round copper discs.

    Our own are deeper.

    We give the rats a little more of ourselves every day
and feel happy, satisfied, the way we should feel
after proper catharsis.

    They become more skilful after a while, more conditioned
or intelligent
                 until we wake up one morning after a sleep
full of bits of earth, droppings, faint scratches, shreds
of newspapers and murmurings of desire
to find the rats looking different, sitting outside their cages
staring at us, pink eyes flat with black light
like watermelon seeds or mirrors.

They must think of us as models also, objects that move,
warm shapes with a smell who fiddle with coloured rods,
metal treadles, component blocks and yellow cheese.

They want us to feed them more of these tricks.
A wire cage and a slice of tomato.
They want to be intelligent like us. They enjoy development.

They represent our aspirations, like 12th-century angels
that consume us and become autonomous.

## How the South Collapsed

The South collapsed slowly after the civil war.
It collapsed into its legislatures and small towns.
The blacks moved into the labour force and low wages.
The governors talked about states rights and became populists.
The good old boys moved onto the front porches of general stores.
Bottles of corn liquor appeared in the back rooms of post offices.
New mills and hardware stores moved into the towns.
Segregation became violent.
Young women went to work in the mills and became wilder.
Good new boys from the hills came down to work in steel
companies
and wander the streets staring at cars and getting drunk at night.
The South didn't participate in the roaring '20s.
They had copper stills but they didn't have New York gangsters.
Hot times in the hotels but very few modern Flappers.
The vote for women came late in the South.
The black southern church became stronger.
White share-croppers were photographed standing in front
of tarpaper shacks.
The New York banks had ruined the South again.
America entered the war.
Southern boys got congressional medals of honour by the dozen.
They were crazy.
They went right over barbed wire fences and blew up German tanks.
The South settled into the '50s.
New industry began to appear, distributorships, agencies.
The South became a dark mirror of America in the '50s.
America riding into the mirror on freedom rides.
The South became new fundamentalist.
The angry subjects of its dead kings.
The populists began to compete for the general electorate.
Washington and Lincoln and Cady Stanton enter the dark mirror.
What is most fundamentalist?
What is most fundamentalist is the rights of the individual.
What is most fundamentalist is reasonable wages.

## Arkansas

I was lying in bed with several pillows under my head
tired after a long day of looking at the lake
the semi-eastern 1920s architecture of the CNE grounds,
all the old houses along Dunn and Tyndall fading to sleep,
their new Polish landlords walking around in their dreams,
a beautiful completely naked woman beside me talking
about children. I went to sleep for a minute
and dreamed my grandfather came in the door
tall and straight with his white hair freshly washed
that he took me by the hand as if I were a child
and led me into the old streets of Brooklyn and Washington
rail cars streaming past in the distance like shining gasps.

Then I opened my eyes and looked at the blue curtains
and the streetlights outside our bedroom.
My friend turns on her side and asks me if I'm asleep.
"No," I say, "I'm awake," and I tell her about the dream.
She bends over and takes me in her mouth for a second
short dark hair blue eyes earring on one ear;
I kneel gazing down at her strong back
the long white lines of her arms and legs
the rye still warm in our mouths on our shoulders
and the dream still present,
my grandfather closing the curtains
and walking out with his suitcase under his arm.

"We have to go to Arkansas," I tell her, wet and erect,
stroking the smooth curve of her sex,
"we have to go by train and explain the separation of powers,
the nature of injustice      how ideas happen in history,
then we can have a child
fresh bread for supper
marigolds      asparagus
and everything will flow from reason as it did in the dream."

## The Promised Land

Our parents used to tell us about it when we were children
it was out there on the other side of the railway ties.
America was a history of success.
Both uncles went south and did well and returned sane
saddle shops and small foundries in Buffalo and Detroit.
Only Duncan went big but lost everything on the orange farm
and returned to Galt penniless but dignified with his service
                                    revolver and steel prints.
Our teachers described it to us when we were in high school
it was a jackdaw a menu a brochure
it was somewhere in the dark on the other side of the lake.
The baseball games were larger and needed Canadian pitchers
the Chicago Cubs needed myself and Neil Pilon
the geography was a kaleidoscope as compared to east & west;
every foundry worker and dentist and streetcar driver
was descended from the tree of Washington's enormous heart.

SDS posters described it as the new black-shirt Germany.
I sold construction equipment and opposed the war in Vietnam.
I read constantly and wrote a novel.
The summers go by and the winters and the days.
Capital falls off and the big companies relocate like groundhogs.
We dream of cities where they pile money up like garden lettuce
sweet Niagara apples and Florida oranges without markets.
I am irritable and long for a publisher as large as Rome.
Buffalo is on the other side of Lake Ontario.
Everyone in Buffalo is drunk.
The same trains still go south and the same conductors punch
your ticket and yack about the Giants.
Approximately half the people of North America are sad.
Duncan, zayda, you and my mother are an influence like headache
despite all my experiences,

you are like a birthmark under my left arm the inside of my thigh.
The promised land still opens up for me as large as an ocean
a green plain of farms hotels iron works and dazzling
                              glass mezzanines

where there will be strawberries and blue grass and Jeremiah
where the water will be cleaner and the steel bluer
where the missiles gleam in concrete silos
where the birds eat peanuts
where my mother's mother more beautiful than any silver print
by Steichen is waiting for me at a downtown Washington park
twirling her blue parasol
where the capitol buildings are Egyptian
where the post-office walls describe Oregon
where we will all be free
men and women will have equal relationships
children will be born speaking Latin
the northern rank and file of the mine workers will decree salary
the meek will pass judgment on the rich
the lost photographs of my father's father will be found in
                              Mazatalan
where all my troubles will be laid to rest like bitter dust

**Permutations**

There was a fine rain that day.

We came off Yonge heading west on Bloor
directing traffic at all the intersections,
your hair damp, splashes on your red dress,

And stopped for some hot soup, lentil and bean,
in that restaurant with the wooden tables,
the one they tore down, or was it
the Italian bakery across the street,
or that little Greek place
where we used to get dalmathes on the second floor,
last summer when you packed
your bags
        and went to Montreal?

## Goodbye: A Photograph in Advance

In my favourite photograph
you are always planting things

Chipping at rocks
and measuring trees. Usually

You are wearing faded chinos
and an old shirt

Tattered enough
to wipe your hands on. You

Are more beautiful than ever
the restraint gone from around

Your mouth. In the dark green
of the photograph your

Steel glasses
burn like fire.

## Unemployed Again So Desperate

The first bank overcomes me totally. I shove
the 5 x 7 note across the counter and stare deeply
into the teller's eyes like a hypnotist from a '40s film.
She stiffens and looks at me out of her attractive face
as if I were a bright figure about a hundred yards away.
"I have a gun," I tell her, and bring the right-hand pocket
of my jacket up to rest on the bakelite counter.
"All in hundreds," I explain, "I don't want a farce
full of loose money stuffed in bags."

She returns with the money, glancing from side to side,
adjusting the collar of her red and blue striped blouse.
"One more thing," I add calmly, "lift your skirt up
to your hips and just stand there without saying a word."
She stares at me in disbelief, eyes widening, mouth parting.
"Pull it up to your hips," I tell her, "it's like love."

She takes a deep breath and lets it out, closes her eyes
and slowly brings the grey tweed skirt up to her hips.
"Higher," I tell her, "I want to leave with you looking
like the Statue of Liberty at midnight."
The pulse beats in her neck and she pulls the skirt past her hips.
Terrific legs no stockings and garters etc but great.
"Good," I tell her, "I'll remember you better than the bank."

She screams and I walk out quickly,
a quiet handsome young man with a lot of aggression
and a set of car keys in his free hand. All I've ever wanted
was to write great poems and meet beautiful and exciting women.
Paris by Thursday. The sun shines. I leap into the stolen car.
Fifty deviant policemen spread out in the city of dreams
to begin their public-minded search while I depart.

## Metro Roads and Traffic Department Menu

Plump freckled Elaine shows us her blue thumb
while I cut my first piece of the cafeteria's best
veal parmegian in weeks. Her crazy son slammed
the car door on her hand but is a free-style swimmer.
Insurance companies are vultures with the teeth of sharks.

Carol idly puts the knee of one voluptuous leg against me
while Maureen interrupts Elaine's moaning
to tell fey and balding Allan he eats too much starch.
She shakes her long curly reddish hair
and continues munching a serving of potatoes.

All the moans and cares of the world begin swirling
along the surface of the cafeteria as I finish my meal
and pause for a moment to reflect on the nature of unionism.
Elaine doesn't like her supervisor.
Allan wants to go and work for a tobacco company.

Maureen sorts through her purse for a cigarette. Allan
talks like a dreaming tomato about his imagined sexual prowess.
Carol moistens her red mouth and gets up and leaves.
Elaine and Maureen put their warm arms around each other
and weep for the gross injustices of the world at large.

The sparkling young Filipino dietician comes over
and asks me how I'm enjoying my lunch: excellent, I tell her,
just excellent: all the repression piled up in one elbow,
cock stirring vaguely as the tall blonde lawyer from Assessment
comes past, and I turn back to my coffee and a fresh lemon
                                      tart with meringue.

## Poles

A number of years ago I saw an issue of the women's magazine
*Aphra.* There was a section of photographs in the issue
and one of them showed a row of public urinals in the shape
of women with their knees drawn up to their shoulders.
There was a man standing in front of one of them wearing a
tan raincoat and urinating between the woman's urinal legs.

We live somewhere between Tennyson's sensitive poem *Maud*
with its subtle control over language, its wide livingrooms
and readily available garden, and that picture turning up
at times to haunt us in black and white.
How many times did the real Maud draw her round white knees
up to her shoulders and with whom?
She smiles at the idea: Tennyson, the crippled Victorian,
in a tan raincoat in public urinal?
                                        But sometimes we find
ourselves caught in flight and tumbling like a wounded bird
in the direction of that photograph. To fall in what?
A human urinal cluttered with cigarette butts & bits of paper?
These are extremes.
I have no idea what kind of perfume the real Maud wore
although Anthony Hecht in his poem *The Dover Bitch* suggests
that Arnold may have taken his lady friend bottles of
                                        nuit d'amour.
Perfume and urine are debatable.
Children piss on each other as an innocent game.
Some of the best French perfumes smell like lighter fluid.
The nakedness of the body is innocent or at least simple.
The nakedness of the body is emphatic but limited.
The nakedness of marriage is more beautiful and also
                                        more terrifying.
The real nakedness of marriage is like an operation on the heart.

**Being Loved**

To be loved because I am gentle or brilliant—

What merde.

I would rather be loved for a Lamborghina,
for a white linen suit
or a restaurant that serves an acceptable Coquilles St. Jacques.

Have a bodyguard who accompanies me
to concerts and corporate mergers,
a .44 magnum under his arm, a dark suit
and a matchstick between his teeth.

This at least would be simple.

There would not be any confusions.

I would not have such terrible headaches
as I slam out of second-floor bedrooms
into these dark hallways full of nothing

the light at the bottom of the stairs alive with birds.

## Shoulders

The strength of women's shoulders is a social reflex.

Not the slightly bunched strength you see reaching
for a box of papers on top of a semi-abandoned sea-captain
bookcase
              but the invisible strength with the resonance of a cello
that you see supporting your body
in the evening light of bedrooms,

past the rapid scherzo of orgasm into the long minutes
that follow,
              as if there is an effortless trick
by which our weight and momentum can be made to float
like a bruised swimmer with a torn mouth
who pauses at night on the calm waters the deep lake
inland from the violent coast
where the mud eel coughs at all our broken dreams.

## Knees

     I tell myself I am happy but my knees disagree.
They stretch in the corner and sleep like dogs.

     At night they devour bad blood like oatmeal or bran
and sniff the wind; slowly they are learning to breathe
by themselves while the body walks up and down

     a bare floor in the sunlight.

     Night leans in at the window and blinks a moon face of death.

     Old black hat with a handful of pits.

     My ambivalence is like a fist. I bend the thick fingers
and release a dead child, a crocodile, a man with a gun.

     There is satisfaction in this and a kind of peace.

     The dogs look up at the body, growl, and go back to sleep.
They are feeling stronger now. Their mouths are red.

     The blood with the oatmeal clicks in the brain
and their dreams pass into the night
like trucks swerving into control at the approach of a bridge.

## Bogart

Another dull evening sitting here listening to a French poet
who thinks Stéphane Mallarmé is a form of source material
and Roland Barthes is the perfect application, a scalpel, say,
with which to do one perfect thing to each Mallarmé gesture.
What to do about the state of literature and these boring people?
Go home have a cool shower read a good autobiography.
Too tired to suggest anything to the girl in the red dress.
Typing too much every day; drinking too much at night.
Go home make some tea read a great book about Napoleon.
Some Italian recipes or a history of Portuguese trade routes.
Maybe a comic novel with some picaresque plot changes.
Maybe a history of the car in North America.
Napoleon. Napoleon was attractive and interesting.
Napoleon amounted to something. Napoleon became important.
My mother would have respected Napoleon.
Short stocky rugged dark absolutely determined pivot of history.
These people commenting on commentaries are syphilitics.
Not even a geographer's general historical view of a pebble.
Idiots. Pretenders. Cretins.
What ever happened to the traditions of French surrealism?
What ever happened to Daniel Fuchs?
Is Kenneth Fearing dead or living in a hotel room?
Dark night quiet mist pleasant stars in a night sky.
Bay & King looks like a canyon of cubed light.
The Queen streetcars run all night.
A cool shower a good sleep and sort the new book tomorrow.
Have lunch, drinks, make love, go to the Art Gallery.
Mañana.
The French have become boring. And the English also.
Everybody in Nebraska speaks Polish.
A good breakfast on Thursday go out in a raincoat like Bogart's
with some Camels and rob a bank; no shooting etc no shooting;

just walk out with the money feeling clean and relaxed
for the first time in months,
a sunny day      a mild day
a raincoat, dark glasses and thinking about Napoleon.

## Cripples

Cripples have special rights in the democracy of the world.
Their broken hearts and missing arms make a soft rose
and blue charcoal glow like an aura.
Children make fun of them but children are cruel.
Friendly policemen give them rides on cold winter nights.
Many cripples are stoic and cheerful about their infirmity.
They sit on park benches in summer and talk to each other
in voices that float back and forth in the tobacco air
like small brown bulldogs with crimson tongues.

Cripples are the opposite of serious accident victims.
Real cripples are an advertisement for the viability of nature.
Emotional cripples are different.
Emotional cripples don't know what to do with what they've got.
Emotional cripples have something wrong with their minds.
They have a pale yellow bruise in the hypothalamus.
The streetcar has flown out of the tree in the mind.
Shock treatments should be discouraged.
Shock treatments cripple.
Emotional cripples need fresh air and lots of exercise.
They should not be given large problems to solve.
They should not be accused of eating with the wrong fork.
They should not be asked to articulate their ideas.
They should be understood by remote sonar telepathy.
They should be allowed to take ducks for walks on leashes.
They should not be allowed to get married.
They should not have children. They should have blue fish.
They should have the blue fish of the mind.

Emotional cripples don't believe the tree moves in their mind.
They believe their mind moves because the tree is unjust.
They should be given red and blue balloons full of helium
for the purpose of transporting perceptions to the work-bench
of ideas.

They should be kept at the far end of the park.
They should not be allowed to disturb the children.
They should not be allowed to disturb the anatomy cripples
reading their papers and drinking wine on the benches.
The anatomy cripples stretch and lean back against the trees.
The sun filters through the clouds.
The geese float down and stare at the drinkers' calm expressions
and honk like the lawful voice of parks and missing limbs.

## Emily Dickinson's Horses

All the horses she owned in her field of poems are black
tall graceful part Arab horses from Essex
geldings or colts is never clear
the question not raised let alone resolved
these are horses of life but also horses of death
carriage horses that pull phaetons
saddle horses that dance at the edge of meadows
at the edge of her mind before the poem begins
at the edge of her mind where her mind paused
                              and put in flowers
these are silent horses but they scream roses
2-year-olds is unlikely
2-year-olds are green
3-year-olds are larger but ambivalent
these are 4-year-olds with a knowledge of life

these are the male horses of her imagination
and even these are only mentioned from time to time
tall graceful part Arab horses from Andalusia
colts that masturbate against the fence of their stall
broad-shouldered percherons that pull carts wagons
                              or heavy ploughs
rose rose rose     symbol of life of the mouth of female
sex the pink lips petal on petal but as durable
as shoulder or hand
these are silent horses more stately than visiting princes
but they kick down fences stall walls dig up wooden floors
frustrated with anger or confinement masturbate compulsively
distrust other (male) horses but make friends with goats
                              or rambunctious sheep dogs
emily emily emily my sister retiring upstairs with a plate
of celery and cold sliced potato
wet under your stiff white dress stolen from nuns

dark hair coiffed back in a neat roll your teeth gleaming
the face of a young boy stoned on Seville brandy
you rose in a white dress you green colt with small breasts
english professors with dandruff on their tweed jackets
glyph through the milk-white gypsum notebooks of your life
but never meet you standing at the top of a stair
with the light from a small landing window striking across
                                  your huge dark eyes
and your tongue moving suddenly in your pink mouth
as you sense one of these horses starting up in the green
meadow outside your house and outside these poems
where you trapped death like a piece of mica
fragment of black obsidian
and tossed him under the hooves of these horses
these 4-year-olds restrained by carriage traces
released from box stalls
let loose on dirt roads
these wild-eyed responders with a single rose between their teeth

**Positions (1)**


This is one of the most beautiful positions of prayer,
the woman lying on her back with her arms at her sides,
knees raised, legs spread almost casually, eyes open, blue,
and the man kneeling between her legs, her body swimming
in his mind, part angel and part tree, his hands resting
at her knees, equally ready to give his mouth to the
perfect lips of her sex or to fall like a branch
between those thighs where the arch of her body supports him.

Her hand moves like a dove with strawberries in its bill.

If he lies back now on the bed and she kneels across his thighs,
her hair tumbling around her shoulders, one hand circling his cock,
about to fall over him like a cloak, a river, a mouth of flowers,
like the angel of light embracing darkness and making it word,
what will he hold in his hands above her head
except roses, and the invisible antlers of a stag?

**Positions (2)**

1) legs spread almost casually, eyes open, blue
2) they make love in the bathroom with their shirts on
3) he enters from behind while she drifts off to sleep
4) there is no such thing as a perfect sentence
5) she humps his left hip while he reads a manifesto
6) he dreams of an elevator in Denver
7) she smashes dishes
8) they go for a walk in the snow
9) he throws flowers at her for being unfaithful
10) she kneels across his thighs like a mouth of bourbon

## Brothers

*For Toby MacLennan*

He sits here huge and half-naked at my table
wearing a rough tweed jacket, the breast pocket
full of flowers, a loaf of bread in one hand a slab of cheese.

Every time I put my white hat over my heart
and reach for another drink, the brawling flouter
snatches up my glass and drinks it down.

Proust was a pale man who couldn't fart.
Puccini wrote circuses for princes. Lorca said no in roses.

The fat man, my other self, drunk and brawler,
keeps me sober while I reconstruct

What Mackenzie King thought about Kansas
What my mother ate for breakfast the day King died.

## Ascending Image

      he should at least
hit a ball into the outfield
or a line drive
for the pitcher to catch.
                            for christ's sake
tell him to begin with something
we can see
             like an act of god
moving in the blue air above the stadium.

      otherwise
                 why does he bother?

## What Men Have Instead of Skirts

Women do lovely dramatic things with skirts.
They lean over desks and the skirt clings under their buttocks.
They sit in large old-fashioned armchairs and cross their legs.
They stand naked in front of cameras with their skirt folded
                              over one shoulder.
They flip their skirts up at the hip and straighten their underwear.
They come downstairs in a black spaghetti strap and you wish
                              they were naked.
Skirts are attractive     they come in different colours and lengths.
Women make conversation with skirts     they express themselves.

Society differentiates clothing although we're almost the same
underneath except for genitals.

Most men have great legs but they don't wear skirts or dresses.
Malaysian men wear sarongs     Scottish bagpipe players wear kilts.
Most men wear trousers and jeans and shorts and jockey briefs.
Men wear torn cotton windbreakers and play baseball for the Giants.
Men wear trenchcoats and carry .45 automatics under their arm.
Men have enormous shoulders     men are cool.
Men kick each other in the face in fights and drink bourbon.
Men have power and enjoy playing with it.
Men have enormous shoulders and drive Volkswagens.
Gunfighters don't draw from the hand     they draw from the
                              shoulder:
shoulders are essential and function between heart and head.
And underneath we're like you except for a difference in strength.

Stereotypes are terrific     stereotypes make everything clear.
Maybe we're not different enough when we get undressed;
maybe you should have three eyes and I should have a tattoo
                                    on my cock.
Maybe this system was okay before it became so confused.
Skirts are interesting     I like skirts     skirts are great.
Maybe I'll wear a dress to work on Monday.
I've got fairly interesting genitals myself.
A loose dark red dress with a tweed jacket in case it gets cold.
These differences are variable. Maybe I'll carry a shotgun.
You can wear anything you want.
Just tell the banks to lock up their money.
Tell them to put a row of managers in front of the vault.
My Volkswagen's parked in the street.
These enormous shoulders of mine are starved for power.

## Why Canadians Born in Canada Aren't English

Modigliani didn't become French when he moved to Paris.
Cosmopolitan doesn't mean exclusively French.
There have always been les Anglais puritans.
Some ambivalent Germans. A few Dutch. A savage Basque.
Modigliani didn't begin to paint like Manet.
Amadeo had a vision.
He wanted the irregular oval woman to become international.
Gertrude Stein didn't become French when she moved to Paris.
Gertrude Gertrude became an American living in Europe.
She began to write the historical shape of America.
It looked like 27 rue de Fleurus.
Paris has classic traditions and excellent wine.
Most Canadians born in Canada think of themselves as English.
The history of British Law is conducive.
The English are hearty and respect the Royal Family.
This distracts various European visitors
who have met Canadians at European hostels and bars.
They're surprised by our American newspapers and films.
Disappointed we don't control our own steel companies.
That we sell large quantities of natural resources south.
They are foolish and think we should keep them.
For what?
They don't understand we're more American than Hatty Green.
The Americans have botched being American.
The Americans are old hat.
We should make films about our railways.
We should make films about our stockyards.
We should make films about our grainyards.
We should make films about our small towns.
We are the best Americans
and we have been practising in the bullpen of the north.

We have more trees and more nickel and more copper.
We have more water and we slander the Queen of England.
The Lakes are our Lakes.
We are the best Americans and we have the best hockey players.
We are more resourceful more imaginative more integral.
This has been decided from Halifax to Vancouver.
Those great ports on the way to Bermuda and San Francisco.
We are the best Americans.
We are the new honchos.
Life is as calm as an Appaloosa.
                              And then to the south
there is the Paris of Buenos Aires      the madness of Chile
the hot air the moths the great stone Incan temples of Peru.

## Semen

Women are the mothers of children.
Men are the fathers of semen.
Milky white essence of cells & hormonal vitamins.
What happens to all the semen we ejaculate?
So little of it turns into a child.
Who would want 30 children a month?
Think of puberty.
Think of the 12-year-old boy with 180 children.
How could they all look like him anyway?
The semen moves through bathroom fixtures &
garbage cans & sewer gratings where people
have thrown away condoms;
it moves in small pools about the size of a tablespoon
serene as thick rain but rich in molecules of energy;
it moves at different times of the day
through cities like Niagara Falls & New York & Denver,
the wonderful cities of the new world
where women bear children
& men go to work every day
& women often go to work every day as well
up to the ninth month at which point they stay home
& relax & listen to music & drink twice as many eggnogs.
All these wonderful cities of North America
where women have complex emotions about the nature of female,
her image both Venus with children & accomplished vocationist;
& men go to work every day & feel lonely
not often & not at any specific time of the day
but lonely sometimes when they think of their work
& their accounts & the air they breathe & children
not lonely for the love of woman
but exasperated with offices & lonely for the love of fields.

Men threw themselves into agriculture 6000 years ago.
They loved it. Carried it forward. Built huge farms.
Love of land. Of ploughing. Of harvest. Of ripe wheat.
We are lonely now not for the fields or for women
but for feelings of greater life.
Our semen goes into the land & into rivers & into the sea.
Millions of tablespoons of cool milk.
We produce sponges vermilion seaweed small plant life.
We are the fathers of purple sponges & orange plant forms.
We are the fathers of ocean life
& dispossessed from fields
& happy with the manufacturing of orange milk cartons &
gear shifts & computerized forms.
We are the fathers of plant life & milk cartons.
& children, like ourselves once, are the children of women.

Every night we make love there is a single moment after
orgasm when the young boy in me turns around & I lie over you
larger than you are & on top etc & turn my mouth
to your nipple while you stroke the back of my neck. Then
I get up & make drinks & change albums. Music. The dark
bitter rich frothy cappuccino of the Archduke billowing
out like smoke. The strawberries out in the damp fields
brilliant red with green leaves against the earth. Music
is easy. Rivers are white. We talk about fields.

## Nobody Discovers the Theory of Relativity
## While You're Sitting at Work


Poincaré discovered a new theory of numbers in a dream one night,
Archimedes discovered the vortex while sitting in a bathtub,
Cézanne discovered the basis of Cubism in French barns,
but nobody discovers the theory of relativity while you're
sitting at work with payroll sheets spread out on the desk.
People discover themselves and what they've been working on.
Husbands discover they've always wanted red wine dinners.
Hemingway discovered a new theory of prose by watching
the clochards and fishermen by a small island in the Seine.

People discover themselves by being open and cognizant
but nobody changes your life while you're sitting at work.
You change yourself after working all day by having a shower
supper green beans and two scotches in front of the television.
You change yourself by reading about Poincaré and his stupid
                                              numbers,
by imagining Archimedes in the bath contemplating his cock.
You change yourself by beating up the salesman next door
for making a pass at your wife who invited him in for a drink.
You change yourself by reading Hugo's novels on a vacation.
You change yourself by moving to a new house with a back yard.
You change yourself by buying a great dane for the back yard.
You change yourself by buying a Cézanne print for the west wall.

And the world changes you when the great dane bites a small child
when your wife leaves you for an actuarial turd from London
when your father dies at 49 without a professorship
when the Chinese students take over the French embassy in Peking
when you go to Vancouver and look at the wide Pacific
when your first novel is published and you appear on the
                                    Tom Snyder Show

when it rains when it snows when it hails when the sun comes out
when the Chinese students give the French embassy back
                              to the French
when your wife comes back from London pregnant rueful the same
handshake freckles and says that she's still in love.

**True Love Isn't Hard to Find**


One of the most beautiful things that can happen
between a man and a woman lying naked in a large white bed
her tawny hair falling over one shoulder      lamplight
the man erect, an intent satyr, kneeling in front of her
one of the most beautiful things that can happen
between this idyllic couple      is a mortadella sandwich
piled thick with tomato and sweet pepper on caraway rye
the sandwich split in half and eaten between them
the way she pushes her hair out of her eyes and takes
a first bite      blushing slightly and laughing as she swallows
not using the back of her hand as he does but the tips
                                        of her fingers

he eats faster than she does and is finished first
rubbing the muscle in his left shoulder and gazing idly
at the tent of white sheet around her knee
a small piece of red pepper has fallen on his cock
she bends over gracefully holding her hair back with one hand
and picks it off with her raspberry pink tongue
a train whistles somewhere in the night sliding west to Regina
the man stretches out with one leg over her left knee
and begins to read a book on the history of Canadian railways
the woman rumples his hair      picks up several more crumbs
and sits with her arms around her knees      listening
                              to the sound
of the crickets dark and manic in the white snow outside

## Alfred Jarry in Boston

Alfred was invited to read at a Boston Legion Hall
where there were supposed to be some people interested
in his work.

What they expected from Alfred was a history of ideas
a history of France a history of art something erotic.

Alfred read a statement about hypocrisy a statement
about honesty a statement about the fall of Plato.

Then he took a piece of raw meat out of his pocket
and proceeded to eat it in front of the audience.

The audience was shocked.

They expected art.

A member of the audience asked Jarry about God
about America about the Midwest farms about the rivers.

Jarry said there was going to be a war in Europe.

The audience thought he meant the crusades.

Jarry finished the meat and walked out leaving his address.

Walked out muttering and brushing off his dark suit.

These Americans, he said to the doorman, they have money,
a great country, good looks; but how do they expect to meet

Angels? They have no appreciation of art as dark surprise.

## Driving in from Muskoka Slow Rain Blues

Vulva always means something. It always means the mouth
out of which a particular child emerges or may emerge.
It always means the mouth which may understand emotional
reality better than history.
History is serial.
I feel your absence like a total image,
like a knife in the morning shower because I am not erect,
because your body is somewhere else,
because the cock swings relatively useless without you
to give it meaning, focus,
without a child to swing from it like an explosion of flowers.
Sex is both simple and complex.
The ego relates to macro and rages over typographical errors.
I had this insatiable desire while you were in Montreal
to produce a thousand erections,
this crazy desire to buy a dalmatian puppy and call it my child
give it a name like Albert and ask you to make it breakfast.
Beef sausages & eggs with Dijon mustard.
The desire for the cock to be panaceaic and permanent
as 1967 Ford cars that never rust in the winter
or run out of gas on gravel sideroads
outside of anonymous cities like Chatham or Sarnia.
As if there was a cock inside the cock
which I could let down with the hot water and white suds
                                    and allow to play
like a child or a lizard or a goofy puppy;
call the dog Gerald, names aren't always important,
call it the dog principle if you like, dog days, or dog soldiers,
dog papers, the portrait of the artist as a young        ,
a boy and a       , dog nights, dog bones, dog fight, dog kiss.

But let's not talk about puppy love or playful or schlemiel
because this dog is a bitch and a bastard, a cunt and a schlong
Sometimes love is a dog.

I phoned Randy long distance and asked him to come in for drinks.
What else are brothers for?
He said, David, you're always drinking too much and breaking
windows.
The morning shower is better.
That feeling of something turning around in your balls,
like a vertebra or a murmuring heart,
a cock the size of a tree and a cunt like a red barn,
to let the raw meat come down in the quiet light of evening
with all its uncommitted violence and sappy love like clowns,
let you touch it with your blue eyes and feel the grind
of brown honey burning like a chicken in the mouth of a dog
laying omelettes scrambled with salami and cheese,
just simple chemistry, just simple science,
biology is wonderful and biologists can explain anything,
like the slam of sweat and honey in the heart
when you lose a sentence of breath
speaking the glossolalia paragraphs of the perpetual outsider
thinking about the distance between motivation and goal,
seamed ball and net basket;
torn shorts and a frayed jockstrap third since Labour Day,
the night they carried you off the basketball court
into what seemed like an endless parade of cars and cold beer
pretzels that cracked in your mouth like farts
blonde girls who smelled of soap and toothpaste and roses
whose armpits tasted of Ban and copper
and your life seemed as simple and perfect as one of the cars
driving down the 401 with a map laid out on the dashboard,
blue lakes with red and yellow lines for highways
that shimmered in the dark and promised you would be a success
the baskets would always be north and south
the rules would always be intellegible
love would always mean love
anger would always mean anger
the fouls would always be visible
the cars and pretzels would be as endless as the night

## Strachan Avenue

The first factory I worked in down on Strachan in the '60s
reflects more changes than the new Constitution.
Maybe it always did.
Calvin, 40 this month, a shop steward, twice in Kingston,
is the best picket organizer in the plant.
Allan was laid off twice during his first 6 months
once for rote and once for pushing a foreman around
but is back on permanent and a member of the executive.
Paul dropped out of an honours program to become a machinist.
Jean paints and goes to Spanish community demonstrations.
Bob reads *Playboy* but likes cooking.
Nobody reads Proust.
Nobody likes management.
Attitudes go back and forth like a softball.
Mel disagrees with everybody but defends the union
and hands out pamphlets on economics.
The new blue-collar milieu makes the university look reactionary.
Sceptics wary of marriage but married with 2 children.
Pat who thought the Church ripped him off as a child
used to spit on nuns in the street and piss on the steps
                          of cathedrals
but would loan out his last 5 dollars in the rain
is casually honest      because he doesn't have a degree in law.

Consistent fundamentalists on questions of natural logic
who don't own businesses and look forward to slow days of work
a hot shower dinner family pork chops with yellow corn
who are experts on nothing and therefore can face empty night
who can face nada
who are the most organized area of the population
divided in their response to next week's peace march

but exact on the number of broken thumbs in a single factory
who tend to believe in dichotomies:

| two kinds of women | stuck-up | and | friendly |
| two kinds of men | assholes | and | regular guys |
| two kinds of jobs | back-breaking | and | unemployment |
| two kinds of art | abstract | and | descriptive |
| two kinds of money | nothing | and | somebody else's |

who make me feel affected when I use unnecessarily long words
who are out there whooping and shouting on Brador and Blues
                                 and cheap rye
normal organized restless diverse industrial workers
who are the dark storm building up on the horizon
that is obviously not part of the weather

## Louis Armstrong's Handkerchief

Louis Satchmo Armstrong used to have a trick when he was
a young man & starting to make a splash in the clubs
the locked-door speakeasies & the black after-hours spots;
he used to put a handkerchief over his right hand while
he played some of his most original melodic solos,
& explained himself after the band took a break
by saying, "I don't want those other musicians
to steal my stuff." His stuff was important. His
originality. His breaking down of the English hymn
& popular song structure into bourbon jazz. He didn't want
the other musicians like Bix to take away or pick up on
his particular work, heart, his heart, of which he had a lot,
beating in his own 2/2 time & wanting to sign its name.
Another way of saying you can share the meal I'm eating
but don't fool around with my head. Louis was a poor boy
as are we all & wanted to make it in the big cities of New
York & Paris. Men are like this about women sometimes.
About imagined infidelities or lapses that are not that much
more important than imagined infidelities anyway.
They're afraid the lapses will interrupt the pleasure of being
reassured by somebody who acts like a partner. An ego
partner. A body partner. A partner in quiet drinks after
evening love-making when there is no one else but the two
people & the bed still warm & rumpled from the moving around
& the cold sharp rich drinks (whoever invented ice-cubes
was also some kind of genius, a Norwegian perhaps sitting
around in the back room of a small factory & drawing diagrams
of freezer coils on sheets of brown wrapping paper),
some clothes on the back of a chair & some books open
on a table & the large window with some distant traffic
& the moon. A body partner. A social partner. John down
the street didn't mind his friend Allan not paying back
the 500 dollars for 6 months but went red blind with rage

when he walked into the kitchen & found Allan kissing
his wife in the middle of the half-lit kitchen floor. Men
are like that or at least the historians or history say we are.
Women are also perhaps but less given to screaming & outraged
vocal expression. Women are more socially constructive anyway.
More tuned to children. Pick him up before he gets into those
tools you've left on the floor. This is simple & not a
limitation. But Louis Satchmo Splendiferous became mellower
as he got older. He became mellower as he made records
that were distributed through stores & played on large Victrola
gramophones. The solos were recorded & dated & filed in their
neat envelope covers. Louis Ambitiousdellamostus became a bit
mellower. He had gone into the clubs & come out with his hands
full of yellow flowers. He could drink a little now & think
about Paris & Amsterdam. Men are often like this about women
but women are different. The body partner. The social partner.
Tawny & blue. This is someone you can't play solos with
every night of the week.

## Potatoes

This poem is about the strength and sadness of potatoes.
A calm vegetable unknown in Chinese history
and never mentioned in King James's version of the Bible;
an earth tuber, plain dusty brown,
passed over by the Indians who preferred the bright yellow
of corn, its sweetness, the liquor they made from it,
pemmican and wild corn mush.
Potatoes and corn have many uses.
The potato was seized upon by the more spiritual Puritans
while their companions were enraptured
with New World tobacco and cotton and squash.

The Puritans recognized earth in the pale potato.
Its simple shape reminded them of the human soul.
The many eyes of the potato amazed them.
They split it in half and saw the indivisibility of man.
They looked at the many shades of the potato
and saw God looking back at them with the colour of light.

Potatoes enjoy many different kinds of soil, resist cold weather,
store well in cool cellars and are more nutritious than beets.
Potato dumplings became the pièce de résistance of eastern
                              Europe.
They developed a considerable number of useful proverbs.
For example: "Love is not a potato, do not throw it out the
                              window."
Or the famous Scottish lament–"What good is he to me?
For three days he has not even brought me a potato."

The potato is modest and develops its crisp bounty
under the ground; it takes colour from traces in the soil
and just enough skin to resist an excess of moisture.
It can be harvested easily by young boys and girls working
in rows with bushel baskets and pausing at lunch
to lift up their skirts and make love under the fences.
Truckloads of potatoes can be sent to every part of the world.
The French make *frites* with them. The Russians make vodka.
The Chinese have rice and North America has potatoes.
Potato flour is not as sweet as corn but makes an excellent bread.
The potato saved Ireland while the English gorged on mutton.
The cellars of poor farmers all over North America
have potatoes stacked quietly on top of each other growing eyes.

## A Poem About Poland

Poland is everywhere.
The machinist we've invited to supper has a missing thumb.
The electrician next door is a shop steward.
There is some cold chicken with lemon on the table.
Ideas are aired. Some music plays in the next room.
The machinist relaxes, the tension goes out of his neck,
we break open a bottle of the wine he has brought.
Appellation controlée Bordeaux.
Four of us are graduate students,
Paul is in marketing,
Debra does freelance design jobs,
Allan is a union organizer.
I am the only writer in the room and work at a nothing job.
We talk about events of the last few months,
look at a book on the history of presses,
discuss the structure of different gears
and the difference between strike breakers and the police.
We add some experiences of our own.
Paul puts forward the idea that strikes are expressions
                                    of consciousness,
John makes a few points about the role of students.
I restrain my desire to talk about the darkness of Stendhal.
My friend June is wearing a gorgeous red cotton shirt.
The machinist is cogent and practical.
The conversation circles around. There are personal vectors
where a man's heart turns into a flower, a stone, a stream,
and back to heart again, pumping like a self-contained
red lake in a pink and brown sky without any algae or fish;
there are country fields and Winnipeg railway tracks
where an unemployed carpenter walks alone at night
thinking about great families and the history of soldiers
under a clear moon.

A young woman in a white dress walks
through the old walnut doors of the room and refers to a
French composer by his first name. Paul is amused.
I forget who I am at this dinner.
A cockroach scurries across the table and the worker
tosses it casually but not insensitively onto the floor.
Glasses are emptied, plates stacked:
I want to go home and look up Gdansk in the phone book;
the nine of us walk into the garden and sit on the grass
the women folding their skirts between their legs
while the men spread their jackets; coffee and cigars
                                        are passed out.
The machinist is tired and wants to go back to his hotel.
History is full of simple events.
I should have been shot six years ago      in the middle of a
                                steel workers' strike.
Put a newspaper over my face.
I have been reading too much about the history of drills.
Practical knowledge is the foundation of general ideas.
Practice is everything.
Definition is orgasm. Everything. Now the weather changes.
Gardens are comfortable. The night is warm
and dark and cicadas cry. We sit talking while one of the
(I am trapped with these people by my inability to speak
                        a properly synthesized english)
women smokes a long black cigar and two of the men play
cards for another bottle of cognac.

## Hound

Hound is liver-coloured and smooth after his evening run
laps up the bowl of water in the half-lit kitchen and sits
licking his lips as the shirtsleeves man drinks coffee.
The maples outside are yellow and most of the flowers are down.
He stretches like a sleek single muscle under the table
and points his long head at the ceiling lights the doorways
opening into the cool air and whiter light of other rooms.
This is the quiet moment at the slow close of every evening
looking out over the city hazing south and west
the big neon signs turned on for the night and the rough country
stretching green and brown to the north past tractors and
                                        groundhogs.
When he hurls himself against the door he makes the catch rattle
in the lock and the garage in the gauze curtain tilt sideways.

People who don't know anything about animals say that dogs are
reflexive and can't experience a contemplation of what they see.
Dogs have no names or causal index for things.
A factory is a series of dark rooms and smells of grease.
Dogs do a lot of the same things people do      eat run sleep
fall in love fart take an active interest in the world.
People eat work sleep get married and drink too much.
What fascinates me when he sits staring out over the yard
is the way that chicken gravel car tree announce themselves
without index cards and more fluidly than they come to me.
Calm is as calm as the wind rustling through trees in a poem
but the desperation in the eye of dog is more human than salesman.
The shape of a tree in his mind is large and green and wet.
He knows my feet shoes I wear baths and the way I walk

more thoroughly than a friend or the men and women at work.
My hands have no secrets from him my pockets are shadows
where hands disappear from time to time and come out naked
smudged sweaty grains of tobacco empty since water and food
especially giblets liver the ends of a roast are kept in kitchens.

He follows me sometimes at a distance sniffing the wind ground
air and wherever I go is a definite point on a four-dimensional
map that has no words or tags or exploded diagrams.
The shape of a fire is enormous but contains images that
are discrete and pass on to meadows rivers gravel driveways.
He knows my thick voice when I have a cold or a cigarette.
Dog is a museum of perfect objects banked in chemical reflexes.
My body is my body.
I am lonely without him and the yellow air of the kitchen goes dull
until I hurl myself at the door and go out on the back porch
to gulp the air put the garage right side up wet tree on cheek.
He sits intent crooning tail wagging head quick as traffic
wants to run down chickens and thinks this behaviour on my part
is as shadowy as my pockets and not sensible like dark or light.

## A Note on the Text

The following poems appeared in *The Blue Sky: Poems 1974-77* (Black Moss Press, 1977): "Ascending Image"; "Being Loved"; "The Blue Sky"; "Family Reunion"; "Goodbye: A Photograph in Advance"; "Letter to the Mountains"; "Mars"; "White Rats." All have been revised here.

The following poems appeared in *Dangerous Crossings: Poems 1978–79* (Black Moss Press, 1980): "All the Beautiful Young Men"; "Alfred Jarry in Boston"; "New Age Confusions"; "Beavers"; "Brothers"; The Fire-Bombing of Dresden"; "For Joan Miró on His 85th Birthday"; "How a Writer Should Explore the Nature of Fashion"; "Knees"; "Making It in the City"; "Metro Roads and Traffic Department Menu"; "Permutations"; "A Poem About Poland"; "Poles"; "Positions"; "Potatoes"; "Rustic"; "Satie at the Disco"; "South American Sailors"; "Stepfathers"; "Sweet Cotton"; "Trains"; "Traffic"; "Unemployed Again So Desperate." All have been revised here.

Some poems previously unpublished in book form have appeared in: *Canadian Forum; Poetry Canada Review; Aurora; The Oxford Book of Canadian Verse; Waves; An Anthology of Canadian Literature in English* (Oxford University Press); or have been broadcast on CBC and CJRT Radio.

Printed in Canada